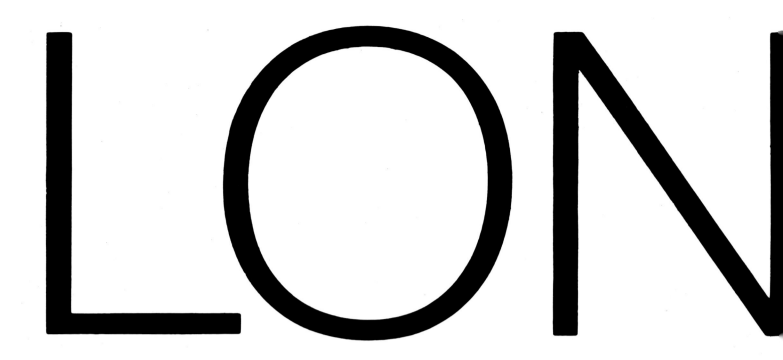

THE GREAT LONDON

STREETS

PEOPLE

OLD BUILDINGS

TROOPING THE COLOUR

GLIMPSES

LIGHTS

This edition published in 1984 by
Bison Books Corp.
17 Sherwood Place
Greenwich, CT 06830

ISBN 0 86124 190 8

Printed in Hong Kong

Reprinted 1990

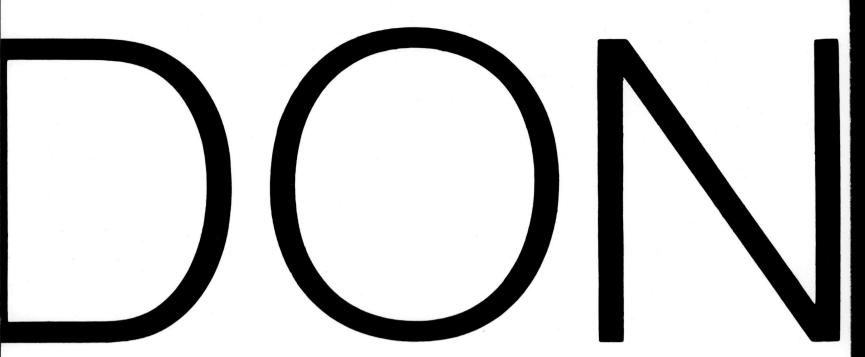

DON

PHOTOGRAPHY	MARCELLO BERTINETTI ANGELA WHITE BERTINETTI
TEXT	VALERIA MANFERTO DE FABIANIS
DESIGN	MARCELLO BERTINETTI ANGELA WHITE BERTINETTI

BISON GROUP

to our parents

The authors gratefully
acknowledge the help of Gianna
Manferto, Carlo De Fabianis and
British Airways.

Preface

Few towns have been, like London, the target of so many clichés, of rough and superficial descriptions, of more or less gentle lampoons. And yet few towns have the essence of London, a spirit and a heritage that is as old and as vital as it is vulnerable. A proud but charming city, London is subject to the eye of the beholder. London lives a hundred different lives, showing a myriad of faces all linked by the common thread of its grand historical tradition. A visitor to London, like myself, perceives only a few of the city's many facets, and even these are sifted through one's own cultural background and sensibility. Can England's greatest city be captured and distilled into one grand impression? Can you step into the same river twice?

I myself have had the chance to visit London many times during different stages of my life, but each time a changed city greets me. I was no more than a curious little child the first time I went to London. I was as impressed by the airplane trip as by the city, for my enthusiasm far outweighed my knowledge of London's majestic monuments and grand history. And the people of London? They were nothing more than obstacles to me as I ran through the streets, gawking at shop windows, pressing through crowded markets, watching the lights come alive at dusk. It was autumn and I remember it rained quite often. Everything looked so big, jutting up through the gray sky! I can still feel the rain bathing my face as I raised it to look at The Houses of Parliament's spires or the windows of Westminster Abbey.

The next time I arrived in London was a few years later, after graduating from high school. I felt apprehensive, somehow sure that I would be disappointed. But my fear quickly dissipated as a different city greeted me, one as changed as I was myself. I was no longer an eager child, and London was no longer so full of surprises. But the loss of instant receptivity was replaced with a deeper appreciation.

I tried to explore the town methodically to get a broader and more impartial perspective. But this approach proved frustrating, as London lent itself to a preordained order no more easily than I did. After a while I found myself wandering along the streets without a particular destination or schedule. It was then that I began to discover the day-to-day life of the city. And I discovered the people, who appear reserved at first, but who are really open-minded and extremely nice. A different and exciting London was coming alive for me.

It was the period of the hippies' peaceful protest and Piccadilly Circus was crowded with an incredible collection of characters. Someone played guitar in one corner of the square, while a throng of people celebrated the moment with dance. Close by, a colorful, long-haired group listened to a speaker talk about peace. The bobbies, London police, watched the happenings discretely, while indifferent gentlemen crossed the square. In Piccadilly Circus different ways of life coexisted, or even better, enhanced each other.

The idea of London as traditionally austere and somewhat severe was supported by London by day. But when evening fell the city let down its hair, bursting into a new life. Music flooded the streets every time a night club door opened. The lights took possession of the streets and squares, and an almost feverish shudder ran through London. We could be as giddy and as wild as we wanted; we *were* the city.

When I recently visited the city again, I hoped to renew the images and feelings of London that I had carried with me from my previous trip. But again, when I arrived on that hot June day, everything looked different. Had London changed? Or had I changed? I reflected on these questions as I stood in Parliament Square at dusk. A quietness seemed to grow as the sunset ushered in a strange play of shadow and light, enveloping the ancient buildings and seeming to alter their very shapes. My eyes half-opened, I followed the outline of the buildings' spires, silhouetted by the vanishing light. As evening approached, the avenues and parks became animated and the branches of the trees leaned out and withdrew, moving with the cooling breeze. I had never seen London enveloped in such a warm, red light.

In Piccadilly Circus as well, the waning light softened the grotesque masks of the punks, today's protesters, replacing the hippies of yesteryear. When night finally arrived I walked along the familiar streets, looking for old pubs. I climbed into the top of a red double-decker, letting it carry me all around the city while I savored the night spectacles. The London that I knew so well was elusive at the same time, as ungraspable to me as if I were a stranger.

Now, as I sit at my desk, I know that when I return to London I will always find a different town, fraught with old memories but filled with new impressions. No matter how familiar, London is an ever-changing reality that shows itself little by little. This dramatic and personal city can only be approached directly, through sense and feeling. London cannot be introduced in words, but is best encountered in person or in a series of beautiful pictures which have to be interpreted by each person's own fantasy.

Valeria Manferto De Fabianis

The Great London

Talking about London means first of all talking about its most famous and impressive features, its main streets, its most important buildings and monuments: The Houses of Parliament, Trafalgar Square, Buckingham Palace. As a matter of fact, these are the real core of the city, which over the centuries has developed in an area little more than a square mile.

Two thousand years ago, London was nothing more than a huge swamp close to the River Thames' mouth. In the year 43 AD the Romans built the first stable bridge, more or less where the London bridge now stretches. Since that time, London has not stopped expanding, through both prosperous and troubled times. Today, Greater London consists of 32 boroughs and encompasses some 620 square miles.

Every day in this growing city, almost 800,000 people travel to work on London's 7000 buses, over 40,000 subway cars, and 380 trains. Almost 22,000 bobbies operate in the city of 7 million people. For so vast a city, though, London retains a distinct charm with its historical architecture and its relatively high degree of civil order.

17 Designed by the Austin Motor Company, the London taxi is both distinctive in appearance and comfortable to ride.

19 In the foreground, the Tower Bridge which was opened to traffic in 1894. It consists of a double drawbridge, which is lifted only once a day early in the morning. From this bridge you can enjoy the best view of the Tower of London and its typical Norman structure. The Crown Jewels are today safely guarded in the White Tower, the oldest part of the Fortress, built by William the Conqueror.

20–21 On the right the Blackfriars Bridge. Built in the second half of the nineteenth century, its name derives from the Dominican Friars, called 'Blackfriars' because of their dark cloaks. In the background the lit dome of St. Paul's Cathedral, which looms 366 feet high.

22–23 In the center of the picture of Nelson Column dominates London's historical heart in Trafalgar Square. Raised in 1843 to celebrate the victorious battle of Trafalgar, the Corinthian style column with a statue of Admiral Lord Nelson atop reaches a height of 170 feet.

24 Looking east along the River Thames, one can spot first Lambeth Bridge, then Westminster Bridge and finally, the Charing Cross railway bridge. This beautiful view of London shows the city's sprawling dimensions.

25 The most famous and impressive buildings of London cluster by the River Thames. In the foreground by the river, The Houses of Parliament and Big Ben, and beyond that, Scotland Yard. Across the street from The Houses of Parliament stretches the beautiful Westminster Abbey —the coronation church of British monarchs and the burial place of many eminent people. Beyond Westminister Abbey one can see the majestic Whitehall.

26–27 Westminister Bridge, completed in 1862, stretches across the River Thames from the ornate spires of the Houses of Parliament.

Streets

a

b

52a–52b–53 Quiet interludes in the park. London people take pride in their well-kept parks, where anyone can escape the noise and rush of the city streets to relax with a book or newspaper, or have a little snooze.

54 The network of London's streets is extremely complicated, which is why the city taxi drivers must undergo difficult examinations in order to become certified.

55 This lady's charming outfit represents typical English formal attire—white gloves, pearls and a jaunty hat.

56 Many Indians reside in London, reminding one of the years of the British Colonial Empire.

57 Speakers' Corner, a small area near Marble Arch in Hyde Park, is reserved for all people who want to preach their opinions and feelings to the public. Especially on Sundays, this place is crowded with impromptu speakers challenging passers-by to get involved in a variety of issues.

58a The waterfront of the Serpentine inside Hyde Park is a favorite lounging spot for London people. According to legend, Peter Pan lived on the lake's island.

58b London's punk population is alive and well. The punks, adorned with tatoos, eccentric hairstyles and startling fashions, usually loiter in groups in particular areas of the city, sometimes even charging a fee to be photographed by tourists.

59 Richmond Park, once a royal preserve, still harbors about 600 deer. The park also contains The White Lodge, seat of the Royal Ballet School.

Old Buildings

The heart and soul of London reside in the rich variety of architectural styles of its historic buildings. From the ornate to the austere, London's landmark buildings testify to the city's long and fascinating past, keeping alive the city's grand tradition.

London's evolution from a big feudal village to a lively metropolis is well-documented in the stylistic continuity of its buildings over the last few centuries. From the austere severity of the monolithic London County Hall to the rich Gothic structure of Westminster Abbey, London's old buildings represent aesthetic and cultural values through the ages.

Even today, careful urban planning with an eye toward neo-classic design has preserved London from the architectural mishmash afflicting other rapidly growing cities. London's buildings are indeed a pleasure to behold.

61 One of the several spires adorning the Houses of Parliament.

63 Almost completely destroyed by a fire in 1834, The Houses of Parliament were rebuilt between 1840 and 1860. Extending over eight acres, the imposing building includes 11 courtyards, 100 stairways, 1100 halls and 10,560 feet of lobbies.

64–65 This dramatic statue of Richard the Lion-Hearted stands before The Houses of Parliament.

66–67 The vaulted ceiling in The Nave of Westminster Abbey, built in the thirteenth century, inspires awe in even the most casual observer. Royal coronations have taken place in the Abbey since the fourteenth century. Many eminent men and women have been buried here, including Mary Queen of Scots and Sir Isaac Newton.

68 The Russell Hotel is one of the oldest and most magnificent hotels in London. Located near the University of London and The British Museum, this Edwardian edifice offers convenient and comfortable lodging.

69 The Houses of Parliament harbor the House of Commons and the House of Lords. The House of Commons was largely rebuilt after the bombings of World War II. The House of Lords is where the Queen addresses both houses at the opening of Parliament, and where Winston Churchill delivered many of his famous speeches during World War II.

70 St Paul's Cathedral is both the tallest and the most famous church in London. Constructed between 1675 and 1710, the Cathedral's dome reaches a height of 366 feet and offers a splendid view of the city. While Westminster Abbey is a church for royalty, St Paul's Cathedral is a church for the people.

71 The London County Hall is the seat of the Greater London Council, which represents and administers all of Greater London's 32 boroughs.

72–73 The dimensions of The Tower Bridge are remarkable for a movable bridge: the middle span extends 70 yards and weighs 2000 tons. The twin steel towers are 200 feet high.

74 A picture of Westminister Abbey at sunset. Begun in 1050, this formidable Gothic structure reverberates with spiritual and historical significance.

75 The Houses of Parliament are adorned with many spires and towers, the most important ones being the Clock Tower and the Victoria Tower, on top of which the English flag flies when Parliament is in session.

74

Trooping the Colour

No other people has as strong an attachment to their traditions as do the English. Their traditions symbolize the continuity between the past, present and future, and the English love for military parades illustrates their respect for the ceremonial. Loyalty to the national flag and devotion to the Queen mix in the most spectacular and exciting of these celebrations. On the first Saturday of June, for the Queen's official birthday, 'Trooping the Colour' takes place. Its origins date back to the beginning of the eighteenth century, when the royal insignia were shown to soldiers just before battle.

More than 1500 soldiers in red uniforms and bearskin busbies march to the sound of drums and bagpipes, recreating the military mood of the past. The Queen herself, riding sidesaddle on a royal horse, inspects the troops. An enormous and silent crowd follows the ceremony, losing the present before the power of the sounds and colours of the past.

77 *During the 'Trooping the Colour' parade, the Queen inspects her troops on her black horse called Burmese, a gift from the Royal Canadian Mounted Police.*

79 *Held annually on the first Saturday in June, the 'Trooping the Colour' parade celebrates the Queen's official birthday.*

80–82 The large Esplanade of the Horse Guard Parade comes alive with colour and sound during the grand spectacle.

83 The parade starts from Buckingham Palace and continues along The Mall to the Horse Guard Parade at Whitehall, where the real ceremony takes place. At the end the troops escort the Queen back to Buckingham Palace.

84–85 The full uniform of the Queen's Guards consists of the typical scarlet jacket and the bearskin busby.

86–87 Each year in June, a huge crowd attends the ceremony at the Horse Guard Parade, for which only 7000 tickets are available. The tickets are drawn from among the many written requests received by the Queen's Chancellor by the end of February.

88 *A spectacular demonstration of military precision, the procession charms and enthralls the crowd as the band plays a traditional song.*

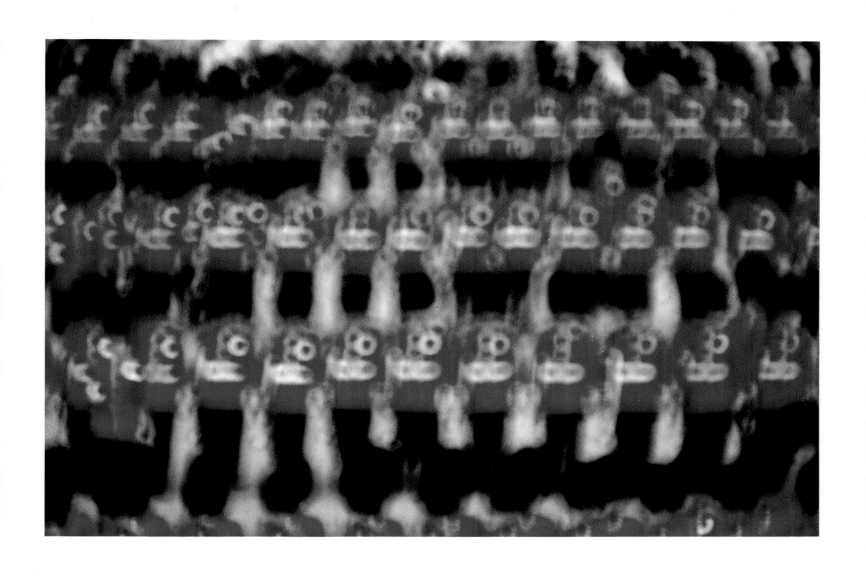

89 A representational impression of the ceremony, in which suggested movement and heightened color contrast dramatize the evocative power of the event.

90 By presenting the insignia to the Queen, the historic moment before battle is brought to life again.

91 The Horsemen of the Household Cavalry, drawn up in the Horse Guard Parade, pay homage to the Queen.

Glimpses

As with all other big towns, London has to be discovered little by little. Only by seeking out and exploring the many little worlds of London—the side streets, the nameless parks, the riverside—can you experience the real London.

Leaving the main streets, you could merge into the bright and colorful confusion of the markets, losing yourself among the many stalls of Petticoat Lane or of Portobello Road. Or you could cross one of the several bridges over the Thames in the damp air of early morning.

Day after day it grows harder to resist the charm of London's anachronistic telephone boxes, the characteristic signs of the pubs, the old-fashioned street lamps glowing yellow at night. And at the very center of London life, the pubs, with their mugs of frothy beer, dim lights and their comfortable décor. Mingling with the crowd, different every evening but always similar in conformation, you could join in a discussion about sports or politics, play darts or follow in the silent meditation of an old gentleman lingering over a pipe of tobacco.

Then, after the last beer, you could emerge into the autumnal air of London at night, when a thin drizzle begins to wet the asphalt of the roads. Walking slowly, savoring the night smells, you will discover the ever-changing city that is London.

93 A sign of one of London's many pubs. A typical and vital English institution, the pubs are, first and foremost, a place for meeting and socializing in the evening.

95 Old-fashioned red telephone booths characterize London's streets and squares.

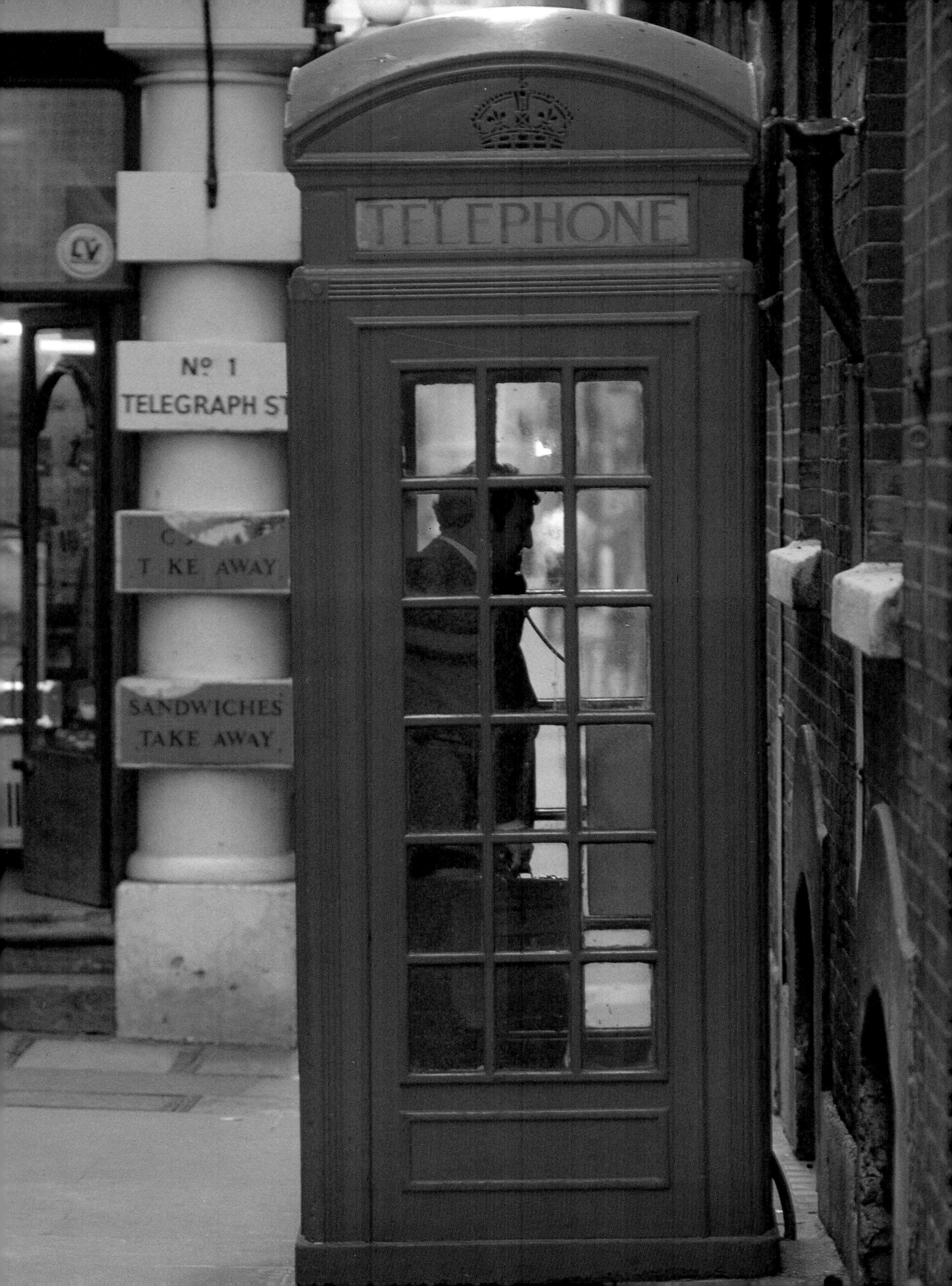
TELEPHONE
Nº 1
TELEGRAPH ST
SANDWICHES
TAKE AWAY

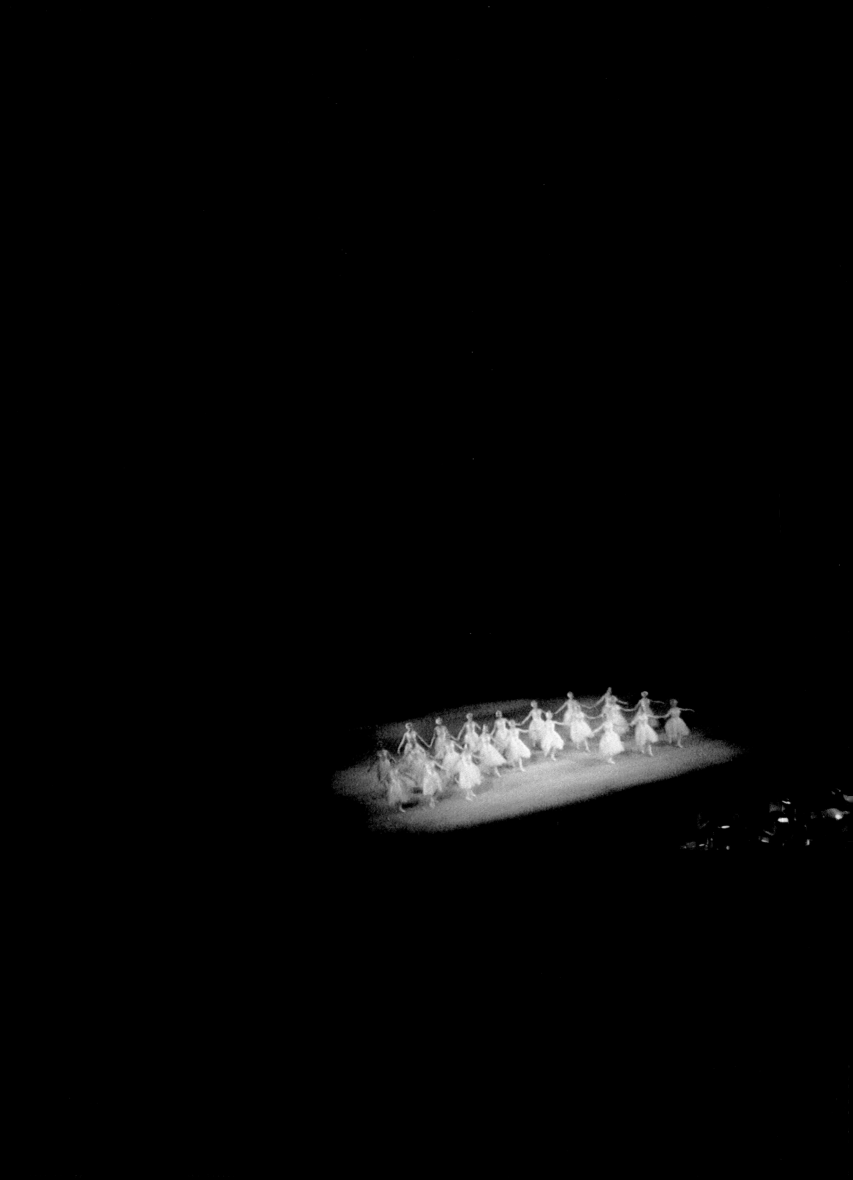

118–119 Silhouetted in the light of sunset, The Houses of Parliament seem almost Oriental in architecture.

120–121 Love of the theater in all its artistic manifestations is a hallmark of English culture. In London large crowds attend the more than 50 theatres nightly.

122 The Palace Theater, which specializes in musicals, can be compared to the most famous theatres of Broadway.

123 Bright multi-coloured lights characterize the night life in Piccadilly Circus.